DRIVING AMONGST IDIOTS

Written and Illustrated By:
Ber t Witte

English Version By:
Herbert I. Kavet

30 29 28 27 26 25 24 23 22 21 20 19 18 17 16 15 14 13 12 11 10 9 8 7 6 5 4 3 2 1

Ivory Tower Publishing Co., Inc.
125 Walnut St., P.O. Box 9132, Watertown, MA 02272-9132
Telephone #: (617) 923-1111   Fax #: (617) 923-8839

INTRODUCTION

This country contains thousands, maybe millions, of miles of roads, paid for by your taxes and all laid out and paved for your personal enjoyment and use. It also contains lots of parking places. Unfortunately, everyone else in the country also thinks the roads are for their personal use, and most of these people, at any given moment, will be on the same stretch of road or want the same parking space you are interested in using.

INTRODUCTION

The worst part is that most of these other drivers on YOUR section of road are total idiots. Since you bought, or were given this book, you are probably not one of them. At least you had the sense to spend $5.95 plus tax to perhaps save your life. But besides you and me, the roads are crammed with idiotic incompetents dedicated to getting in the way of your totally sound driving. There are only two kinds of drivers: those going slower than you who are turkeys, and those going faster than you who are assholes.

ABOUT THE ENGLISH EDITION

This book was originally written in Dutch by the brilliant Dutch artist, Bert Witte. Holland is the most densely populated country in Western Europe, so you can imagine what it is like driving there, not to mention all the leaking dikes. However, the Dutch translation sounded something like this (I am not making this up), "If you intend to start yourself set gear in free. If someone else does it, it depends on a lot of personal circumstances and factor whether or not this is of importance."

ABOUT THE ENGLISH EDITION

This didn't exactly crack me up. The translation kind of reminded me of those early Japanese instruction manuals of the 70's. So in the interest of providing you, my kind readers, with a few laughs (so maybe you'll buy a few extra copies for gifts) I just rewrote most of the book. Also, the Dutch version was filled with all those funny international road signs which no one here understands.

WHAT MAKES A DRIVER AN IDIOT

Basically, the idiot is totally oblivious to pedestrians, cyclists and other motorists who are also totally oblivious of him or her. The police call accidents caused by this attitude "Hit and Run." In actuality, the idiot isn't running. He doesn't even know an accident happened.

WHAT MAKES A DRIVER AN IDIOT

When the idiot has an accident with someone in a larger vehicle who also happens to be physically bigger, the idiot has an easier time directing his attention to the problem. This usually leads to police officials, insurance companies, lawyers and the filling out of many forms, which the idiot doesn't like at all.

AN IDIOT'S BACKING UP SKILLS

As long as cars have reverse gears, you can never feel safe standing or driving behind an idiot. The fins and sharp accessories of the 70's proved to be a leading cause of death in the United States during that era. Fortunately, most of these vehicles have faded from use.

THE POLICE AND IDIOTS

You must have an element of compassion for the brave police officer who directs traffic on busy corners filled with distracted motorists. This is especially true with older idiots who are often the most dangerous. Driving in St. Petersburg, Florida and other retirement communities is an experience most younger drivers do not wish to duplicate. While leaving the scene of an accident is a pretty serious crime, most idiots feel there are some situations where "running for it" makes lots more sense.

TYPES OF IDIOT DRIVERS—
THE CANNED SARDINE IDIOT

This idiot has too little money for the size of car needed. The subcompact he drives has room for his body but little space left over for transporting his brain. The inside mirror lodges itself against his forehead, the steering wheel is under his chin, the gear shift secreted in an unmentionable portion of his anatomy and all this is while he is driving from the back seat.

THE SHORT AND OLD IDIOT

You've seen these drivers every time you go out, valiantly trying to peer over the top of their steering wheel, and every now and then, actually getting a glimpse of the road. This Short-Old Idiot manages to cause an accident every two or three miles and was recently given a last chance by her 16th insurance company. She is greeted very respectfully by her car dealer and every body shop within 25 miles of her residence.

THE MIDDLE-AGED MATRON IDIOT

The Middle-Aged Matron Idiot drives tensely and tentatively with her lower lip firmly planted against the steering wheel as she peers through the windshield, ever fearful that she will miss something. Her body is rigid. Her hands grasp the steering wheel tightly and her top speed is 18 M.P.H. She will stop immediately at any perceived or imagined danger.

THE AGGRESSIVE IDIOT

The Aggressive Idiot is a driver to watch out for, as if anyone ever watches out for any other driver or anything other than police cars. This driver uses his vehicle as an extension of his macho personality, or at least the macho personality that manifests itself the instant he gets behind the wheel. Macho drivers are dangerous even if their car is not moving, what with the horn blowing, finger gestures and threats of homicide.

THE RELAXED IDIOT

The Relaxed Idiot is an idiot if only for his attitude. You've probably read enough already to realize that being behind the wheel is no place to relax. This idiot's position gives a superb view of the sky, birds and tops of trees. It is favored by high speed drivers on super highways, where there is little need to actually view the road itself. Everyone knows a driver like this. In fact, if you make a list of them here, it might remind you to buy each of them this book as a little gift. This relaxed position is very conducive to napping and it is best to stay away from drivers who are in the process of taking one.

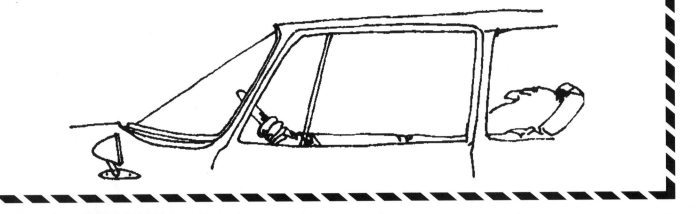

THE NERVOUS IDIOT

This driver feels hunted, which is, all in all, a reasonable concern, and swivels his or her head constantly to convince themselves that they are observing every possible danger. Observing, of course, every possible danger is totally impossible and this makes the nervous idiot even more nervous. The jittery condition of this driver's intestinal system dictates that he or she stop at every rest area.

THE SNOOZING IDIOT

You would hope this idiot is snoozing at a rest area but this is not always the case. Young beachgoers are especially likely to adapt this position to enhance their tan on the way to the seashore. This position is especially unnerving when you notice the amount of beer that is accompanying the group. There is also some kind of law amongst young people about keeping no more than one hand on the wheel when assuming this pose. The other hand is reserved for fondling, opening the aforementioned beer or turning up the volume on the radio.

THE WHEEL-HUGGING IDIOT

No one knows why the Wheel Hugger hugs the wheel. Perhaps there is some sort of sexual stimulation involved. The Wheel Hugger always wears sun glasses, so it is very difficult to tell if he/she is awake. This position is, perhaps, a leftover from the '50's when hot rodding hoodlums would wrap an arm similarly around the wheel because they thought it made them look tough.

THE FRESH AIR IDIOT

This granola type has the windows and sun roof open during winter and summer. Who knows, perhaps they don't close? Arms are carried external to the vehicle to maximize the draft. Usually this nerd has a pipe and wears glasses but for some reason, the artist left them out. This is not a particularly dangerous type of idiot as the open nature of the car makes the driver sensitive to all forms of verbal and physical abuse.

THE CONVERSATIONAL IDIOT

Lacking the ability to induce anyone to drive with him or her, this idiot feels compelled to carry on conversations with other cars at traffic lights, stop signs and often when zipping along at 65 M.P.H. "Hey buddy, you really should have that muffler looked at," or "Say, when did you visit Niagra Falls?" More lights are missed because of people getting dragged into a conversation with this idiot than for any other reason. If it weren't for the healthy condition of the horns in the cars behind, it is doubtful that traffic would move at all.

THE REST STOP IDIOT

This is an endangered idiot, at least in the United States, where this position, when the car is stopped, is an invitation for immediate larceny. Many Rest Stop Idiots awaken to find the front seat the only remaining part of their car. Some teenage idiots may adapt this position to try to simulate the appearance of a jeep, especially when hauling friends in mom's 1987 Toyota.

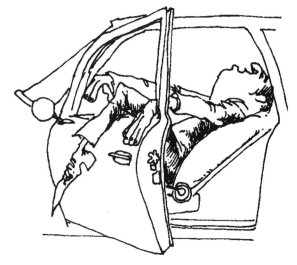

THE NOSE PICKER IDIOT

The most classic idiot driving position, common as dirt and a favorite traffic light pastime. The driver works a pinky, forefinger or thumb around the nasal passages, searching, in his (or her) boredom, for any minute boogers that may have escaped scrutiny at the last traffic light. Often, at least at the beginning of a trip, the idiot is rewarded with a strike and drives on contentedly, anxious to repeat the performance as he disposes of the offending fragment with a FLICK out the window.

THE PET LOVING IDIOT

Never mind the cat and dog hairs all over the seat, this driver should be avoided because of the danger from the animal crawling across the dashboard, wagging a friendly tail in the idiot's face or burrowing contentedly in the cozy spaces between the brake and accelerator pedals. Pets in cars cause more accidents than alcohol and speeding combined. When the insurance companies comprehend this, they will base their rates on the size of the pets rather than on age or accident record.

THE SEX STRUCK IDIOT

This idiot, almost always a guy, isn't so much interested in the sex within the confines of his four wheels as to that which ambles by his windows. The Sex Struck Idiot is easily distracted by any feminine form, and something as stimulating as a short skirt or overflowing bust is almost a certain cause for an accident. Women experience this breed of idiot in bars and at work, too.

THE MAKE-UP IDIOT

Women get very good at this. They can comb their hair, apply lipstick, do eyelashes and eyeliner while easily exceeding the speed limit on most highways. Applying make-up at stop lights is so common, it rivals nose picking as a national pastime. Auto manufacturers cater to this pastime by putting ever increasing numbers of mirrors in their cars. These manufacturers are no dummies and they know the more time women spend looking at themselves in mirrors, the more autos they'll be able to replace.

THE NEWSPAPER-READING IDIOT

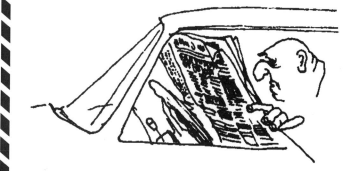

It's bad enough when someone tries to look at a map and drive at the same time, but every commuter sees this idiot on a regular basis. I mean really, how stupid can you get? And I'm not talking about reading at stop lights either. You think car-jacking is a national problem? Newspaper Idiots are really why auto insurance rates keep going up.

THE SMOKING IDIOT

Smoking is considered a criminal act in the U.S. these days, and the privacy of one's auto is one of the last sanctuaries available to the addicts. The guilty feeling, certainly, is still there and most smokers, very surreptitiously, empty their ashtrays in fast food parking lots when they think no one is looking.

AN IDIOT'S GUIDE TO BREAKDOWNS

A car is a very complicated piece of machinery and even fully trained mechanics with certificates and awards and diplomas covering their walls don't have the foggiest idea of what's going on in the real innards. Oh yeah, they can change a battery or muffler and most often replace a wiper blade, but get into fuel injection or electronics problems, and just getting to the broken part will destroy the integrity of six others. Smart owners don't let anyone touch their cars until the thing no longer runs, and then they either sell it or have it towed away for free by donating it to a national charity.

THE COMMUTING IDIOT

Not technically a driver but more of a team. These people spend so much time together that they form sort of a club. It's a club whose members they spend much more time with than their wives, families or jobs. To encourage more of this efficient form of travel, some states have set up special commuter lanes, the use of which is restricted to cars with two or more people. Since there is little hope of enforcing something so silly in this democracy, it merely gives idiots another lane in which to perform mayhem.

THE CONTACT LENS IDIOT

It's just a tiny speck of dirt in the corner of the lens, but the pain is intense, and the Contact Lens Idiot is positive he or she can jiggle the intruder out without stopping the car. When you see a car weaving about as though the driver is blind, you can be pretty sure it's the Contact Lens Idiot. It wouldn't be so bad if the operation could be done with one hand, but you see, you have to lift the lid with one hand and play with the lens with the fingers of the other. All this while having practically no vision and steering with your knees.

WHO TEACHES ALL THE IDIOTS TO DRIVE

Perhaps you've never thought about it, but someone has to teach all the homicidal incompetents you see on the road to drive. Sometimes a family member or friend may be called in to help, but most often, it is a driving instructor. These instructors age very quickly and their families often wonder why they chose such a profession.

WHO TEACHES ALL THE IDIOTS TO DRIVE

The illustration below shows some of the compulsory reactions driving instructors make so their students can know at a glance what they did wrong.

1. Stopped at red light against bumper of car ahead.

2. Passing a police car on a bend at high speed.

3. Jamming on brakes too late to avoid running through window of China shop.

4. Backing up on wrong side of the road.

1   **2**   **3**   **4**

LEARNING TO DRIVE

In Europe, this is how they teach people to drive—well, at least they put that little "L" sign which stands for "Learner" or maybe "Leper," but whatever it is, everyone stays away from a car with that red "L" on it.

LEARNING TO DRIVE

In this country, most professional driving instructors are portly former accountants who sell real estate in between giving driving lessons. These people are dedicated and hard working and teach people to drive just as incompetently and dangerously as they do.

AN IDIOT'S GUIDE TO OPENING HOODS

With unfamiliar cars or rental cars, the opening of the hood can be pretty tricky. Just pushing the appropriate button under the dash isn't nearly enough. Additional safety features abound to prevent the hood from flying up and obscuring your vision, in case you were watching the road in the first place. First rule: Don't force it with your hand, you'll hurt yourself. Use a tool.

AN IDIOT'S GUIDE TO OPENING HOODS

Remember, opening hoods is not the simple task it once was. These things can be stubborn, and the sophisticated idiot knows enough to get a bigger tool and not be afraid to force it. Don't give up.

ATTITUDE

Attitude is always the definition of a <u>real</u> idiot. Any idiot can run over a pedestrian or cyclist. The <u>real</u> idiot continues on as blasè as ever, figuring nothing has happened, and in truth, as far as he is concerned, nothing did happen.

AN IDIOT'S GUIDE TO MIRRORS

It's impossible to drive safely without at least two mirrors, and more will only make the driver more aware of other dangerous idiots overtaking him. Mirrors are also good for checking nose and ear hair growth in men, and for applying make-up for women.

AN IDIOT'S GUIDE TO RADAR DETECTORS

No idiot would think of owning a car without an up-to-date radar detector. Many find it even more crucial than a radio. Not having a radar detector would distract the idiot from making obscene gestures, working his or her horn, playing with the sound system and cutting off other drivers, because he had to waste time watching for police cars.

AN IDIOT'S GUIDE TO AIR BAGS

The driver's air bag will be in the steering wheel. Be sure to keep the steering wheel in front of you in emergencies.

AN IDIOT'S GUIDE TO STICK SHIFTS

All idiots claim that they can drive a stick shift, whether or not they even know where the clutch is. Actually, a standard transmission is pretty simple with the four speeds in an "H" pattern. Reverse, however, is hidden in a variety of places and sometimes you have to lift the whole stick up or push it down or even lift a secret ring thing. Put the average idiot in a five-speed or six-speed auto and his local garage will prosper.

AN IDIOT'S GUIDE TO ARM SIGNALS

The accomplished idiot uses hand signals at random and irregular intervals to direct air streams into the car, dry nail polish, wave to a friend, stretch and occasionally indicate direction change. Idiot passengers do the same.

AN IDIOT'S GUIDE TO RIDING AS A PASSENGER

When riding with someone who the idiot perceives as a less skilled driver than himself, you can be sure he will offer advice or even take the wheel if he feels the situation is serious enough.

AN IDIOT'S GUIDE TO RIDING WITH A PASSENGER

Idiots, on the other hand, are not very gracious in taking advice, and comments about their driving are likely to be received poorly.

AN IDIOT'S GUIDE TO FUNNY INTERNATIONAL ROAD SIGNS

Traffic symbols are inherently unpredictable. One minute they're green, the next red, and they have a tendency to proliferate, showing up suddenly where you never thought they were before.

AN IDIOT'S GUIDE TO FUNNY INTERNATIONAL ROAD SIGNS

1. No playing around

2. Passing forbidden for two cars at same time

3. No soliciting

AN IDIOT'S GUIDE TO FUNNY INTERNATIONAL ROAD SIGNS

No one really knows what those funny international signs mean, at least no one in this country. Probably the foreigners are just as confused; after all, many of them don't even know which side of the road to drive on.

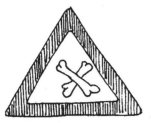

1. Dangerous crossing

2. Share a seat belt with someone you'd like to be close with

3. Bad hair winds ahead, close windows

AN IDIOT'S GUIDE TO FUNNY INTERNATIONAL ROAD SIGNS

I think you are allowed to ignore most of these foreign symbols if you don't speak the local language. This is especially true in countries where they park on the sidewalk.

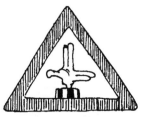

4. Watch out for paper cuts

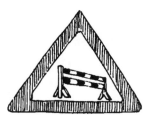

5. Steeple chase zone

6. Use a funnel when pouring wine into your flask.

AN IDIOT'S GUIDE TO FUNNY INTERNATIONAL ROAD SIGNS

1. Earthquake area

2. Undershirts recommended

3. No shoulder, steep-river bank

AN IDIOT'S GUIDE TO FUNNY INTERNATIONAL ROAD SIGNS

1. Steep grade with railroad crossing. 16% blood alcohol permitted

2. Free for all zone

3. Watch out for meteorites

DRIVERS WITH A TEENY BLADDER

I don't know why I'm mentioning it right here, but some drivers have teeny bladders and this is what they look like.

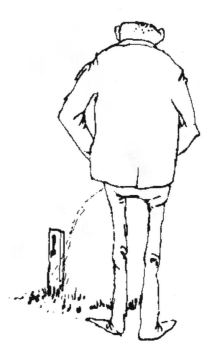

FOREIGN DRIVERS

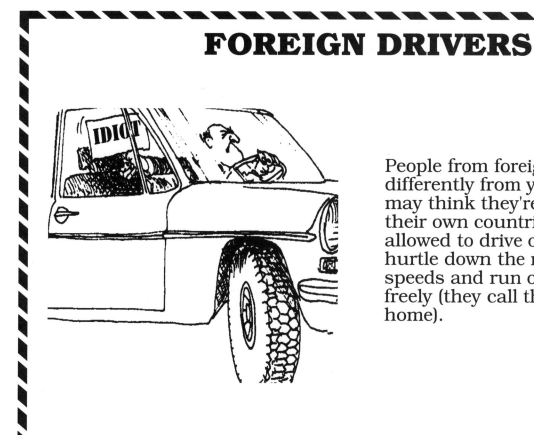

People from foreign countries drive differently from you and me. You may think they're idiots, but in their own countries, they may be allowed to drive on sidewalks, hurtle down the road at incredible speeds and run over pedestrians freely (they call them peasants at home).

HORNS

The horn is considered by idiots to be the most important part of the car. Besides its basic warning function, horns allow idiots to vent anger, hurry up slowpokes and persuade other drivers to stay away. The horn is at its effective best when warning pedestrians to stand clear of the idiot's latest maneuver.

HORNS

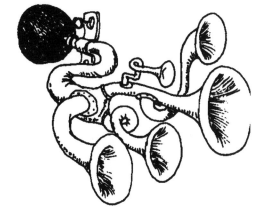

Horns are also wonderful social devices. They have been used by idiots for centuries to help drivers celebrate victories and other happy occasions, as well as greet friends. Horns are also splendid for announcing the idiot's arrival and departure and are especially effective after 2 A.M.

MUFFLERS

"Take care of your muffler or you won't be able to hear your tunes," is an old Greek saying. Actually idiots learn about mufflers only after they fall off, and many find they prefer to drive their car this way. The muffler's main function is to fall off at the most inconvenient moment possible, like before a big date or just as you pull in to get your car inspected.

MUFFLERS

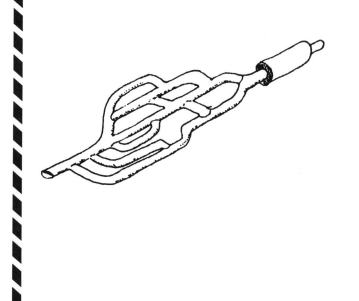

Having your muffler fall off, fortunately, is not much of a problem. Practically every street that cars can fit down have six to twelve muffler shops, run by earnest young franchise entrepreneurs who will, with great sincerity, give you a written estimate and lifetime guarantee, that covers everything for the next time your muffler falls off, except labor and a service fee that cost essentially the same price you paid for the muffler in the first place. Believe me, this is how it works. If mufflers were made to last more than a year or two, there wouldn't be a muffler shop on every corner. These people can't afford to give away free mufflers.

GLOVE COMPARTMENTS & MUFFLER GUARANTEES

Writing about mufflers makes me think of glove compartments which is where you stash your muffler guarantee, along with your tire guarantee and your radio guarantee. I'm sure the companies honor all the guarantees but when something is wrong, all the searching in the world will fail to produce the piece of paper you require. Guarantees must be printed on some special paper that self destructs after 12 months or 10,000 miles, whichever comes first.

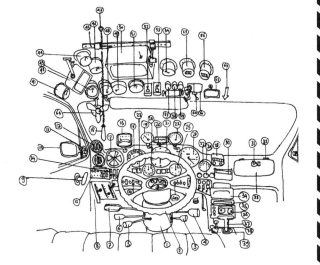

MUFFLERS

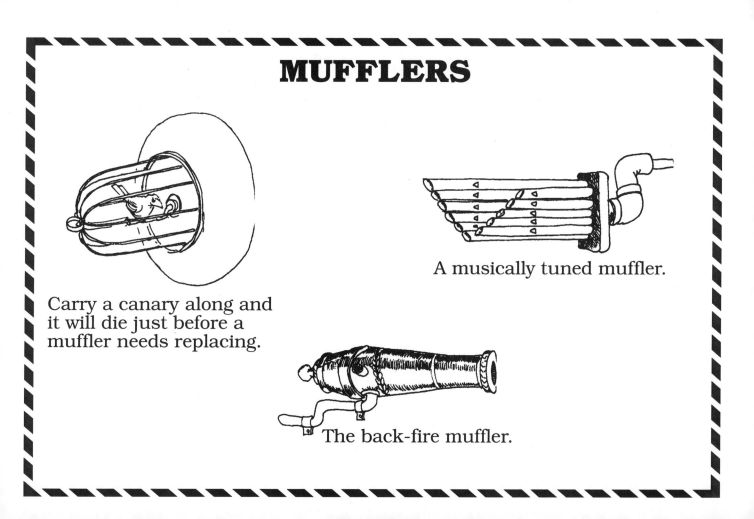

Carry a canary along and
it will die just before a
muffler needs replacing.

A musically tuned muffler.

The back-fire muffler.

UNDERSTANDING OTHER DRIVERS

Every other driver, idiot or not, can be considered a challenger for the same piece of road you were planning to drive on. By learning his or her facial expressions, you will learn about these adversaries and be better able to anticipate their moves.

Leaving
driveway.

Opens eyes for
first time on
entering thruway.

The senses sharpen
as the driver realizes
he must now assert
authority.

UNDERSTANDING OTHER DRIVERS

Mild feeling of guilt at not allowing own mother or other little old lady into lane.

More determined concentration, for picking lanes or cutting off buses. Alert, razor sharp senses cued to any opportunity or advantage.

Shock at being outmaneuvered by that good-looking blond he was planning to smile at.

UNDERSTANDING OTHER DRIVERS

Sudden stop, usually caused by taxi cutting him off.

The blasè look, combined with slowing down as a result of radar detector going off.

The innocent expression. Most idiots reserve this look for the moment they pass a policeman. It also can be used when pulling alongside another auto that they previously cut off or otherwise snookered.

UNDERSTANDING OTHER DRIVERS

"Ha, ha, ha, you thought I'd let you make that left hand turn."

"Has anyone else noticed that parking spot? Can I get to it first if I drive over the median strip? The sidewalk?"

Time check. All "Type A" drivers, and they are 90% of the drivers you'll be concerned with, check constantly to see what kind of time they are making. "Aha, Poughkeepsie Blvd., in only 17 minutes—only 30 seconds off the record."

MERGING

Anyone successfully merging in front of you is essentially calling you a wimp. If you expect to arrive at your destination with any self-respect left, you must accept this as the challenge it is and take steps not to allow even the cutest member of the opposite sex, police car or invalid in front of you.

MERGING

Merging is essentially a bluffing game, and facial expressions play a critical role. Sure it's good to have a beat-up dented car that looks like it means business or a mean pick-up truck, but the cool, confident "Never Notice The Other Idiot Look" is what wins almost every time.

CAR SAFETY

Back in the '70's and '80's, U.S. car makers got lazier and lazier and turned out cars that were not very reliable at all. But this has all changed, and competitive pressures along with government regulations have produced autos that are trouble free. Much of the unemployment these days is made up of former skilled auto mechanics who now have nothing to fix.

CAR SAFETY

To be safe from idiots while driving, it's a good idea to always wear your safety belt. This clamp type is generally acknowledged to be the most secure on the market, though it does take a little longer to put on. It is especially effective when combined with the hair drying attachment shown to the bottom left.

OTHER KINDS OF SAFETY BELTS

This Garter Safety Belt is an intimate alternative to the ugly metal and web belts that come with most cars. It's sold in those sexy lingerie stores at the malls and in the catalogs you get marked "STOP, Sexually Explicit Material Enclosed. Do not open if you are going to call the police or post office," and everyone opens it.

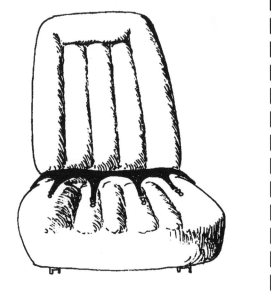

OTHER KINDS OF SAFETY BELTS

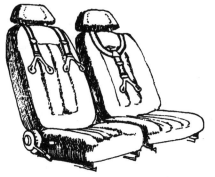

The Suspender Seat Belt ties into those little buttons inside a man's trousers that he never knows what to do with. I don't really know what the Clamp Seat Belt is for, but the drawing was in the original Dutch version of the book so I thought I'd better use it. Don't think it's so easy filling a book about the idiotic things people do when they are driving. The research can kill you!

FUNNY INTERNATIONAL SIGNS

Oh, I forgot, in the section on what those funny international signs mean, this one means "No left turn."

FUNNY INTERNATIONAL SIGNS

The fact that these international signs are universally understood means that people from many different countries can travel safely, always knowing exactly what is permitted and what is forbidden.

THE LAW

Police keep the idiots under control. When one stops you, of course, whether warranted or not, you're more likely to think he is the idiot. But regardless of how justified your actions, the soundest approach is to beg for mercy.

THE LAW

While some places outlaw radar detectors as being unfair to the police, there is NO similar control on police unfair practices. These have been carefully honed by the uniformed protectors of the law ever since the auto was invented.

CAR INSURANCE

CAR INSURANCE

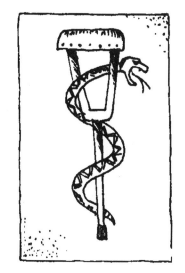

Auto insurance consists of an exorbitant premium that is collected and pooled by very ethical insurance companies, the balance of which, after deducting their own preposterous salaries and expenses, <u>YOU</u> get to sympathetically distribute (if you're lucky enough to sit on a jury), in an enormous lump sum totalling millions (less the lawyer's cut) to some irresponsible idiot, faking a whiplash injury. The inherent fairness in the system is that everyone has a more or less equal opportunity to simulate the whiplash injury.

CAR INSPECTIONS

Many states and probably many countries have inspection requirements for autos. This inspection system somewhat increases the probability that the other idiots' cars will stop on occasion when the brake pedal is pushed and will have a light or two working at night.

CAR INSPECTIONS

The problem with car inspection systems is that everyone who owns a car ancient enough to have some emission or mechanical problem also has a buddy at the service station where the inspection is often done. One hopes that some inspectors are more thorough than in my town, where the inspection consists of:

My Buddy Joe: "Hey, Herb, everything work?"

Me: "Uh, oh yeah."

My Buddy Joe: "That'll be $15."

HITCHHIKERS

Only idiots hitchhike and only idiots pick them up, though of course, we've all done both. If you are the driver, a quick glance at the hitchhiker's luggage may give you an idea of just how much inconvenience the fellow might put you to.

HITCHHIKERS

Another clue to the type of person you are picking up is their attire. This will give you an indication of whether the conversation you may carry on with the individual will be enjoyable as the miles roll by. Although the temptation to be friendly is always there, most drivers find it safer and wiser to just pass the hitchhikers by.

IDIOTS ON TOUR

Experienced travelers know that you can easily survive a vacation with a swimsuit, a couple of pairs of underwear and an extra shirt or blouse. Idiots prefer to haul the entire contents of their closet and garage around with them.

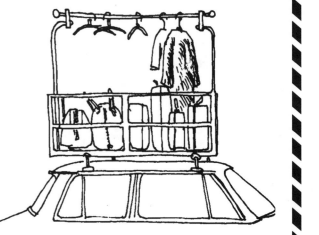

IDIOTS ON TOUR

Carrying too much stuff along means these idiots spend most of their trip loading and unloading their cars and trailers. This is probably just as well, as it frees up the recreational facilities at wherever it is these people vacation.

THE POLICE

Policemen and policewomen much prefer harassing practically innocent drivers than, say, shooting it out with drug dealers armed with automatic weapons or worse. Once you understand this, your relationship with them can be one of mutual benefit. They keep you from getting to your destination too early, and you keep them out of life-threatening contact with dangerous criminals. Only an idiot advises police that he is a taxpayer and his taxes pay their salary and they should be out catching real crooks.

THE POLICE

Most policemen are fair minded and reasonable people, but once a law officer has doubts about the respect you have for his uniform, and once you remind him that his job includes the very potentially dangerous act of going against armed criminals, the consequences are likely to be swift and brutal.

SUNROOFS

Sunroofs seem like such a wonderful idea when you buy your car, but no one ever uses them. No one even opens windows these days, what with pollution and car jackings. You can imagine what could jump into your car through a sunroof.

CONVERTIBLES

Perhaps there are places in the world where convertibles are practical, but in Boston, where I live, it's either too cold or too hot, which leaves about three days in late May when they are fun. The idiots, naturally, are tooling along in 40° weather with the top down, freezing their passengers while they comment on the wonder of fresh air.

AUTO SECURITY

A determined thief can always get what he wants out of your car or the car itself. Real security means having a car no one wants with absolutely nothing inside of interest to even the most desperate drug addict. Having a car like this certainly takes some of the fun out of driving, and most people just take their chances with the thieves and hope they are not in the car at the same time as them.

AUTO SECURITY

Any inner city kid old enough to wear his baseball cap backwards can break into your car and drive it off faster than you can using the key. Security devices may give you some piece of mind, but they only make it harder for <u>you</u> to get in and use the car, not the thief.

CARS IDIOTS DRIVE

<u>BMW</u>—the prestigious yuppy car of the '80's. The BMW originally stood for Bavarian Mountain Water and the company was a brewery turning out a potent dark beer. After the war, when fuel was rationed, crafty German beer drinkers used the beer to fuel their Mercedes. BMW knew a good thing when they saw it and built their entire car around the beer filled gas tank.

<u>Volkswagon</u>—Do they still make these? Whatever happened to the bug and the hippies and the flower filled vans of the '60's? Here was a company synonymous with basic, inexpensive functional, (except for the defrosters) transportation and then they disappeared. Someone said they make golf carts now.

<u>Mitsubishi</u>—I can't help it. Being brought up during the war, all I can think about when I see this car is the Mitsubishi bombers and the Japanese yelling "Banzai," "Kill all prisoners," "Bomb hospitals," "Die *'melican'* nurse," you remember the stuff. It's hard for me to separate a Mitsubishi from John Wayne in a Navy fighter shooting them down.

CARS IDIOTS DRIVE

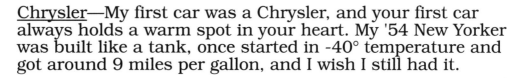

<u>Chrysler</u>—My first car was a Chrysler, and your first car always holds a warm spot in your heart. My '54 New Yorker was built like a tank, once started in -40° temperature and got around 9 miles per gallon, and I wish I still had it.

<u>Bentley</u>—This prestigious auto costs hundreds of thousands of dollars. Few idiots can afford one and by English law, they are sold only to idiots. This is really good because they make only about 23 a year, so if everyone wanted one, they would be very hard to get. Unless you live down the street from a dealer, you'll probably never see one. Actually, my local dealer let me drive one home once but I didn't buy it. I DIDN'T BUY IT!

<u>Porsche</u>—Guys buy Porsches. They're not allowed to be sold to women. Guys buy them because they think they'll get laid more often if they own a Porsche. But women couldn't care less, and it takes so long to get in or out of those things that they end up actually having less sex.

MISCELLANEOUS ADVICE

Never, never drive
behind a sewer truck.

Bucket seats are always
worthwhile accessories.

Bumper crests like this
absolutely terrify
policemen.

Reactive bumpers reduce
damages to your car.

(Anyone who was in Miss Riley's 5th grade class and was assigned a four
page term paper will recognize this page immediately for what it really
is—a filler—hey you think it's easy coming up with 96 funny pages?)

WHERE DO OLD CARS GO?

No one really knows where old cars go. Detroit and Tokyo turn out billions of new ones a year. You happily trade in your old clinker with the transmission about to go and proudly assume 48 months of new payments. The old car? There are just so many used car lots and junk yards. How many old wrecks can suburbanites buy for their au pair girls, or can movie companies destroy in car chase scenes or can Mexico absorb? You know what I think? I think car dealers have secret graveyards where they bury them just to keep their market strong.

THE 10 COMMANDMENTS OF DRIVING

I. *Thou shalt use thy horn freely to express thy opinions of other drivers.*

II. *Thou shalt roll up thy window and lock thy doors when giving truck drivers the finger.*

III. *Thou shalt not have an auto mechanic touch thy car unless it no longer moves.*

IV. *Thou shalt never argue with policemen, but shalt always call them "Sir."*

V. *Thou shalt not believe another's directional signals, as they probably hath been left on all week.*

THE 10 COMMANDMENTS OF DRIVING

VI. Thou shalt realize that other drivers also cannot see in the rain because their wipers are just as worn as yours.

VII. Thou shalt only loan thy car to friends if their deductible is lower than thine own.

VIII. Thou shalt not make left hand turns from the right lane unless thou is very late for work.

IX. Thou shalt learn to expect the lane you leave to speed up.

X. Thou mayest tailgate to inform the driver ahead just what you think of his speed.

Other books we publish are available at many fine stores. If you can't find them, send directly to us. $7.00 postpaid

2400-How To Have Sex On Your Birthday. Finding a partner, special birthday sex positions and much more.

2402-Confessions From The Bathroom. There are things in this book that happen to all of us that none of us ever talk about, like the Gas Station Dump, the Corn Niblet Dump and more.

2403-The Good Bonking Guide. Great new term for doing "you know what". Bonking in the dark, bonking all night long, improving your bonking, and everything else you ever wanted to know.

2407-40 Happens. When being out of prune juice ruins your whole day and you realize anyone with the energy to do it on a weeknight must be a sex maniac.

2408-30 Happens. When you take out a lifetime membership at your health club, and you still wonder when the baby fat will finally disappear.

2409-50 Happens. When you remember when "made in Japan" meant something that didn't work, and you can't remember what you went to the top of the stairs for.

2411-The Geriatric Sex Guide. It's not his mind that needs expanding; and you're in the mood now, but by the time you're naked, you won't be!

2412-Golf Shots. What excuses to use to play through first, ways to distract your opponent, and when and where a true golfer is willing to play.

2416-The Absolutely Worst Fart Book. The First Date Fart, The Lovers' Fart, The Doctor's Exam Room Fart and more.

2417-Women Over 30 Are Better Because... Their nightmares about exams are starting to fade and their handbags can sustain life for about a week with no outside support whatsoever.

2418-9 Months In The Sac. Pregnancy through the eyes of the baby, such as: why do pregnant women have to go to the bathroom as soon as they get to the store, and why does baby start doing aerobics when it's time to sleep?

2419-Cucumbers Are Better Than Men Because... Cucumbers are always ready when you are and cucumbers will never hear "yes, yes" when you're saying "NO, NO."

2421-Honeymoon Guide. The Advantages Of Undressing With The Light On (it's easier to undo a bra) to What Men Want Most (being able to sleep right afterwards and not talk about love).

2422-Eat Yourself Healthy. Calories only add up if the food is consumed at a table and green M&M's are full of the same vitamins found in broccoli.

2423-Is There Sex After 40? She liked you better when the bulge above your waist was in your trousers. He thinks wife-swapping means getting someone else to cook for you.

2424-Is There Sex After 50? Going to bed early means a chance to catch up on your reading and you miss making love quietly so as not to wake the kids.

2425-Women Over 40 Are Better Because... No matter how many sit-ups they do, they can't recapture their 17-year-old body—but they can find something attractive in any 21-year-old guy.

2426-Women Over 50 Are Better Because... They will be amused if you take them parking, and they know that being alone is better than being with someone they don't like.

2427-You Know You're Over The Hill When... All your stories have bored most acquaintances several times over. You're resigned to being overweight after trying every diet that has come along in the last 15 years.

2428-Beer Is Better Than Women Because (Part II)...A beer doesn't get upset if you call it by the wrong name; and after several beers, you can go to sleep without having to talk about love.

2429-Married To A Computer. You fondle it daily, you keep in touch when you're travelling and you stare at it a lot without understanding it.

2430-Is There Sex After 30? He thinks foreplay means parading around nude in front of the mirror, holding his stomach in; and she found that the quickest way to get rid of a date is to start talking about commitment.

2431-Happy Birthday You Old Fart! You spend less and less time between visits to a toilet, your back goes out more than you do and you leave programming the VCR to people under 25.

2432-Big Weenies. Why some people have big weenies while other people have teenie weenies; as well as the kinds of men who possess a member, a rod and a wang—and more!

2433-Games You Can Play With Your Pussy. Why everyone should have a pussy; how to give a pussy a bath (grease the sides of the tub so it can't claw its way out); and more!

2434-Sex And Marriage. What wives want out of marriage–romance, respect and a Bloomingdale's chargecard; what husbands want out of marriage –to be allowed to sleep after sex.

2435-Baby's First Year. How much will it cost, secrets of midnight feedings, do diapers really cause leprosy and other vital info for parents.

2436-How To Love A New Yorker. You love a New Yorker by pretending to understand their accent, sharing a parking space and realizing they look at "Out of Towners" as new income.

2437-The Retirement Book. Updates the retiree on Early Bird Specials, finding their bifocals and remembering things like paying for the book.

2438-Dog Farts. They do it under the table, in front of the TV, and after devouring some animal they caught in the yard. This book describes them all.

2439-Handling His Midlife Crisis. By treating him like a child when he wants to feel young again and consoling him when he goes from bikinis to boxer shorts.

2440-How To Love A Texan. You love a Texan by agreeing that their chili is just a mite hot, humoring them when they refer to their half acre as a ranch and rushing to help when their belt buckle sets off a security alarm.

2441-Bedtime Stories for your Kitty. Kitties love a story before bedtime and this book guarantees to keep their attention; Goldisocks and the 3 Teddy Bears, The 3 Little Kittens, and more.

2442-Bedtime Stories for your Doggie. This book of tales will keep big doggies as well as puppies entranced every night with stories like The 3 Billy Dogs Gruff, The Little Doggie That Could and more.

2443-60 With Sizzle! When your kids start to look middle-aged and when your hearing is perfect if everyone would just stop mumbling.

Ivory Tower Publishing Co., Inc., 125 Walnut St., P.O. Box 9132, Watertown, MA 02272-9132   Tel: (617) 923-1111